Edward Brooks

Syllabus of a Course in Pedagogy

Embracing educational psychology, methods of teaching, school economy,

and history of education

)

Edward Brooks

Syllabus of a Course in Pedagogy
Embracing educational psychology, methods of teaching, school economy, and history of education

ISBN/EAN: 9783337164225

Printed in Europe, USA, Canada, Australia, Japan

Cover: Foto ©Paul-Georg Meister /pixelio.de

More available books at **www.hansebooks.com**

SYLLABUS

—OF A—

COURSE IN PEDAGOGY

EMBRACING EDUCATIONAL PSYCHOLOGY, METHODS OF TEACHING,
SCHOOL ECONOMY, AND HISTORY OF EDUCATION.

—BY—

EDWARD BROOKS,

Superintendent of Public Schools, Philadelphia.

"The object of education is to give to the body and the soul all the beauty and perfection of which they are capable."—*Plato.*

"The object of education is to prepare for complete living."—*Herbert Spencer.*

PHILADELPHIA:
BURK & McFETRIDGE, 306 AND 308 CHESTNUT ST.
1892.

PREFACE.

This syllabus of a general course in Pedagogy has been prepared for a two-fold purpose. First, it is designed as a basis of lectures by the Superintendent to the teachers of Philadelphia on the science and art of Teaching. Second, it is also intended as a suggestion or a guide to such teachers of the city as may desire to continue their educational reading or who may wish to make a more thorough study of Pedagogy than they have hitherto done.

It is to be understood that it is merely a syllabus, though a comprehensive one, and aims to suggest only the leading ideas of pedagogical thought and practice. Details are to be supplied and variations made by the individual student as may be thought desirable. While it is believed that the principles presented embrace all the leading ideas of the great thinkers on educational subjects, from the earliest times to the present day, these are not to be regarded as exhaustive of the subject, but merely suggestive of general lines of thought upon the topics considered. Teachers will remember also that many principles, no matter how broad or comprehensive, will need judicious modification in order to adapt them to the various cases that arise in the actual work of the school-room. It is suggested that the principles given be carefully scrutinized and criticised by those who may examine them, and especially by those who may be guided in their studies by this syllabus. Every professionally educated teacher should have in his mind some such outline of the theory and practice of teaching as is here presented; and it is hoped that these outlines may be at least suggestive of a scheme of educational doctrine worthy of the claim of the possibility of a *Profession of Teaching.*

The Science and Art of Teaching.

INTRODUCTION.

I. The Nature of Education.

1. Education defined and illustrated. Fundamental ideas;—development and knowledge—culture and instruction.

2. Definitions of different thinkers:—Plato; Aristotle; Montaigne; Bacon; Locke; Comenius; Pestalozzi; Spencer; Bain, etc.

3. The problem of education:—Man, the object of education. Matter, the material of education. Method, the manner of education. Relation of the three elements. Divisions which they indicate.

4. Kinds of education:—Determined by the nature of man. Analysis of man's nature. Results of analysis;— (a) Physical education; (b) Intellectual education; (c) Æsthetic education; (d) Moral education; (e) Religious education.

5. Grand aims of education:—Improvement of the individual; development of knowledge; progress in civilization; universal freedom.

II. General Principles of Education.

1. The fundamental object of education is the perfection of the individual.

2. This perfection is attained by a harmonious development of all the faculties.

3. These faculties develop in a natural order that should be followed in education.

4. The basis of this development is the self-activity of the mind.

5. This self-activity has two distinct phases : 1st, receptive and acquisitive; and 2d, productive and expressive.

6. These two phases of self-activity should be carefully co-ordinated in the work of education.

7. There must be objective realities to supply the condition for the self-activity of the mind.

8. The mind operating on these objective realities develops its powers and furnishes itself with knowledge.

9. Education, at a certain stage, should be modified by the different tastes and talents of the individual.

10. A scheme of education should aim to attain the highest welfare of society, the state, and the race.

III. THE BRANCHES OF EDUCATION.

The branches; how determined; their nature and relation; what is embraced in each; general outline of the branches.

1. Methods of Culture:—
   1. Physical culture.
   2. Intellectual culture.
   3. Æsthetic culture.
   4. Moral culture.
   5. Religious culture.

2. Methods of Instruction :—
   1. In language.
   2. In mathematics.
   3. In physical sciences.
   4. In history, civics, etc.
   5. In the arts, etc.

3. School Economy :—
   1. School preparation.
   2. School organization.
   3. School employments.
   4. School government.
   5. School authorities.
   6. School systems.

4. History of Education :—
   1. Oriental education.
   2. Greek education.
   3. Roman education.
   4. Mediæval education.
   5. Renaissance education.
   6. Modern education.

5. The Philosophy of Education.

NOTE.—"Methods of Culture" includes both the physical and mental nature of man. The discussion of the culture of the mental nature is embraced under the head of Educational Psychology, which constitutes the first division of this syllabus. The subjects of physical culture, æsthetic culture, etc., are only incidentally referred to in this syllabus. The expressions, "methods of instruction" and "methods of teaching" are often used interchangeably.

PART I

Educational Psychology;

Or, the Mind and its Culture.

INTRODUCTION.

I. THE NATURE OF MAN.

Man the object of education. Nature of man,—his physical nature,—his mental nature. Relation of body and mind. Education embraces the culture of both body and mind.

II. GENERAL NATURE OF MIND.

1. The Mind :—Its existence,—its nature,—distinction from matter. How to study mind :—by observation,—by language,—by consciousness. Fundamental activities,— discrimination and retention.

2. Value of a knowledge of mind to the teacher :— For its culture,—for its instruction,—for the principles of teaching,—the basis of his work.

3. Analysis of Mind :—Forms of activity, or Faculties. A faculty defined. Classes of faculties ;—Intellect—Sensibility—Will. Their nature and relation. Faculties not parts of the mind—The mind a unit.

III. General Nature of the Intellect.

1. The Intellect defined—Its activities—Its products—The source of knowledge.

2. Faculties of the Intellect:—Perception; Memory; Imagination; Understanding; Intuition.

3. The Understanding (thought-power):—Abstraction; Conception; Judgment; Reasoning.

4. The products of the Intellect:—Ideas and Thoughts—their nature—their origin—their relation.

5. Consciousness and Attention;—their nature and functions.

IV. General Principles of the Culture of the Mind.

1. The object of mental culture is the complete development of the powers of the mind.

2. One of the primary conditions of mental culture is a well-organized and healthy brain.

3. The mind is cultivated by the activity of its faculties.

4. This activity of the mind requires objective realities for it to act upon.

5. Each faculty of the mind requires a culture adapted to its own nature and activity.

6. The culture of the mind should follow the natural order of the development of its faculties.

7. The culture of the mind should aim at a harmonious development of all its faculties.

8. The culture of the mind should be modified by the different tastes and talents of a pupil.

9. The culture of the mind is not creative, but aims to develop possibilities into realities.

10. The ultimate aim of education is the attainment of the triune results of *culture, knowledge, and efficiency.*

THE INTELLECT.

I. The Nature and Culture of Consciousness.

I. Nature of Consciousness.

Its general nature; objects of consciousness; products of consciousness; unconscious mental modifications; development of conscious knowledge.

II. Mental Culture through Consciousness.

Culture through conscious knowledge. Culture through unconscious knowledge. The culture of philosophical consciousness. The culture required for abnormal consciousness.

II. The Nature and Culture of Attention.

I. The Nature of Attention.

1. Its general nature; objective and subjective; positive and negative; relation to consciousness; relation to the will; relation to the acts of the body; number of objects of attention, etc.

II. The Culture of Attention.

1. Importance of Attention:—To perception; to memory; to thought; to genius; to success in life.

2. How to cultivate Attention:—By exercise; by observation; by reading; by study; by mathematics; by natural science, etc.

3. How to secure the attention of pupils:—By manner in teaching; by method of teaching; by appropriate subjects—novelty—variety—interest—adaptation to age, etc.

4. Habits of attention; extent of culture; remarkable examples, etc.

III. The Nature and Culture of Perception.

I. The Nature of Perception.

1. Its general nature defined and illustrated. Conditions of perception ;—body and mind.

2. The Nervous Organism :—The Brain. The Nerves—afferent and efferent. Theories of sensation. Reflex action. The organs of the special senses,—touch, taste, smell, hearing, and sight.

3. Process of Perception :—How we perceive objects. Relation of sensation and perception. Direct and indirect perception. The forming of percepts. Knowledge given by each sense ;—by touch,—by taste,—by smell,—by hearing,—by sight. The relation of sight to touch.

4. Herbart's doctrine of Apperception. Its educational value.

II. The Culture of Perception.

1. Value of this culture. Neglect of culture. Differences of perceptive power. The time for culture. Sense culture the basis of the new education.

2. Methods of cultivating Perception :—By exercise; observing with attention; observing minutely ; object lessons; drawing; natural history; formulas for observation, etc.

3. Culture of the special senses :—(*a*) Lessons to cultivate touch; (*b*) Lessons to cultivate smell and taste; (*c*) Lessons to cultivate hearing; (*d*) Lessons to cultivate sight.

4. Application of Perception in Teaching :—In orthography ; In reading; In geography ; In arithmetic; In geometry; In physiology; In drawing; In modeling, etc.

5. Relation of Perception to the "new education:"—Montaigne—Locke—Pestalozzi—Froebel—The Kindergarten—Object Lessons—Observation and experiment in teaching the natural sciences.

6. The limitation of ·perceptive knowledge:—In history; In geography; In mathematics; In literature; In philosophy, etc.

7. Value of perceptive knowledge:—Its culture value—Its practical value—Errors of the "old education"—Over-estimation of perceptive knowledge—Mistakes in the "new education."

IV. NATURE AND CULTURE OF THE MEMORY.

I. *The Nature of the Memory.*

1. Its general nature defined and illustrated. The conservative faculty. Nature of conservation of knowledge.

2. The elements of Memory:—Retention; Recollection; Representation; Recognition. Discussion of each.

3. The Laws of Memory:—Nature of the laws. Primary laws (law of the permanent idea);—comprehension—attention—feeling—repetition, etc. Secondary laws (law of the related idea);—similarity—contrast—contiguity—cause and effect.

4. General remarks on Memory:—Relation to reasoning—Relation to invention—Memory and old age—Effects of disease on the memory.

II. *The Culture of Memory.*

1. Importance of the culture of Memory. Neglect of culture. Differences in memory. Examples of remarkable memory. Time for culture. Value of the memory.

2. Methods of cultivating the Memory:—Exercise; clear conceptions; attention; interest; repetition; association; special artifices;—verse—key-words—sentences; systems of mnemonics.

3. Application to Teaching:—In orthography—In geography—In history—In literature—In natural history —In arithmetic—In physiology, etc.

4. The Memory in education :—Educational value of the memory—The memory studies—Misuse of the memory in teaching—Rote learning—Words without ideas— Cramming, etc.

V. The Nature and Culture of the Imagination.

I. The Nature of the Imagination.

1. Its general nature defined and illustrated. Its relation to perception. Its relation to memory. Materials used in its operations.

2. Its Products:—new combinations; new creations; their relation and difference.

3. Its Forms:—phantasy; fancy; imagination proper.

4. Its Laws:—Involuntary; voluntary; suggestion; spontaneous; sensible forms, etc.

5. Its Limits:—By space; by matter; by time; by mind.

6. Its Sphere of operations :—Vary the old; combine the old into new forms; create the new,—objects, forms, events, characters, etc.

II. The Culture of the Imagination.

1. Value of the culture of Imagination :—To thought; To science; To poetry; To art; To oratory; To character.

2. Methods of cultivating the Imagination :—By exercise; study of nature; study of art; study of literature; forming new combinations; creating ideal productions.

3. Application in Teaching :—In orthography—In reading—In geography—In literature—In history—In geometry—In drawing—In modeling—In music, etc.

4. Its relations:—To science—To fiction—To poetry—To painting—To sculpture—Idealism and realism in art.

VI. The Understanding or Thought-Power.

1. The Understanding defined and illustrated : names of the faculty; its products ; its operations (analysis and synthesis) ; its basis (comparison).

2. Forms of activity of the Understanding :—Abstraction—Conception—Judgment—Reasoning.

3. Culture of the Understanding :—Its value—Its neglect—Time for culture—The thought-studies of the school—Each faculty to be considered separately.

VII. The Nature and Culture of Abstraction.

I. The Nature of Abstraction.

1. Its nature defined and illustrated. Positive and negative. The power questioned. Arguments for the power. Other views,—limited view, wider view. General remarks.

2. Products of Abstraction :—Abstracts; pure abstracts are particular ; general abstract ideas.

II. The Culture of Abstraction.

1. The importance of correct culture :—Value of the power of abstract thought—The concrete before the abstract—Errors of the old education—Dangers in the new education.

2. Methods of cultivating Abstraction:—By spontaneous activity; drill on abstract qualities; study of the abstract sciences; not take a child to the abstract too early.

VIII. The Nature and Culture of Conception.

I. The Nature of Conception.

1. The general nature defined and illustrated. Nature of the general idea. The term generalization. The term conception.

2. The process of Conception:—The basis of the process; Forming the concept (the three steps); Naming the concept; Forming higher concepts; The three steps not always formal; A synthetic process; An ascending process.

3. The nature of the Concept:—Definition of the concept; Not an image; Relation to a percept; Concrete and abstract; Broad and narrow; Higher and lower; Relation of concepts; Content and extent; Extension and intension; Distribution of concepts.

4. Qualities of Concepts:—Clear and obscure; Distinct and confused; Adequate and inadequate; Notative and symbolical; Absolute and relative; Contrary and contradictory; Positive and negative.

5. Unfolding conceptions:—Logical division; logical analysis; logical definition.

6. Existence of general ideas:—Their existence questioned; nominalism and its arguments; conceptionalism and its arguments; Bain's discussion of the subject; reply to Bain.

7. Classification:—Nature of classification; scientific classification; early attempts and progress of classification; scientific genius; classes in nature.

II. The Culture of Conception.

1. Value of Conception:—Basis of thought; Basis of language; Basis of science.

· 2. Methods of cultivating Conception:—In studies; By logical analysis; By logical division; By logical definition.

3. Application in Teaching:—In geography—In arithmetic—In grammar—In botany—In zoology, etc.

III. The Culture of Classification.

1. Value of Classification:—In common life—To the student—In science.

2. Methods of cultivating Classification:—Classify objects; classify subject-matter of studies; write outlines in studies; study the classificatory sciences; study the principles of classification, etc.

. 3. Application in Teaching:—In orthography; In geography; In history; In arithmetic; In grammar; In natural sciences, etc.

IX. THE NATURE AND CULTURE OF JUDGMENT.

I. The Nature of Judgment.

1. Its general nature defined and illustrated:—Primitive judgments; Logical judgment; The things compared; Analytic and synthetic; Judgments of extension and intension; The proposition analyzed.

2. Nature of judgments:—Definition; Quality and quantity; Kinds of judgment; Relation of judgments; Distribution of terms; Laws of distribution; Substitutive judgments.

3. Derived judgments:—By opposition; by conversion, etc.

II. The Culture of Judgment.

1. Value of the Judgment :—To perception ; To memory ; To thought; To science ; To poetry, etc.

2. Methods of cultivating the Judgment :—Exercises in comparison of,—forms, colors, lengths, etc.; By the studies,—arithmetic, geometry, grammar, etc.; The figures of literature ; Games of skill, etc.

3. Application in Teaching :—In orthography; In geography; In arithmetic; In grammar; In geometry; In manual work, etc.

X. The Nature and Culture of Reasoning.

I. The Nature of Reasoning.

1. Its general nature defined and illustrated. Indirect comparison ; Comparison of relations ; Relation to judgment ; Views of different writers, etc.

2. Kinds of Reasoning :—Deduction and induction ; Their relation ; Kinds of truth to which each is applicable,

3. The syllogism :—Definition ; the parts ; the terms ; the premises ; the figures ; laws of the syllogism.

4. Deductive reasoning :—Its nature ; origin of general truths ; mathematical reasoning, etc.

5. Inductive reasoning :—Its nature ; its basis ; its limits ; criteria of induction ; tests of casual agency.

5. Hypothesis and theory :—Nature of each ; probability ; verification ; origin ; value, etc.

II. The Culture of Reasoning.

1. Culture of Deductive reasoning :—Study of language ; study of mathematics ; study of the physical sciences ; study of the philosophical sciences ; care to avoid the fallacies of deduction,—(begging the question—reasoning in circle, etc.).

2. Culture of Inductive reasoning:—By inductive eaching or studying; by the study of the inductive sciences; by inductive investigations; care to avoid the fallacies of induction,—(of observation, mistaking the cause, antecedent for cause, etc.).

3. Application in Teaching :—In geography; In grammar; In arithmetic; In algebra; In geometry; In history; n natural philosophy; In physiology; In botany, etc.

4. Thought knowledge :—Relation to perceptive knowledge—Higher than perceptive knowledge—Higher han book knowledge—The triumphs of natural science—The triumphs of mathematics—The grandeur of philosophy.

XI. The Nature and Culture of Intuition.

I. The Nature of Intuition.

1. Its general nature defined and illustrated :—Existence of this power; Relation to other faculties; Its products;—Primary Ideas—Primary Truths.

2. Primary Truths :—Their nature; their existence; tests of primary truths; remarks on primary truths.

3. Primary Ideas:—Space; time; identity; cause; number, etc.

4. The subject embraces;—The True—The Beautiful —The Good or Right.

XII. The Nature and Culture of the True.

I. The Nature of the Ideas of the True.

1. Space :—Nature of Space; nature of the idea; origin of the idea.

2. Time :—Nature of Time; nature of the idea; origin of the idea.

3. Identity :—Nature of Identity; nature of the idea; origin of the idea; kinds of identity.

4. Cause:—Nature of Cause; nature of the idea; origin of the idea.

5. Number:—Nature of Number; nature of the idea; origin of the idea.

II. *The Culture of the Idea of the True.*

1. The value of the idea of the True:—Basis of thought; basis of science; relation to art; relation to life.

2. Methods of cultivating the idea:—It unfolds spontaneously. The development of the idea,—of space; of time; of cause, etc.

3. Application in Teaching:—The True in Science—The True in Art—The True in Morals.

XIII. NATURE AND CULTURE OF THE BEAUTIFUL.

I. *The Nature of the Beautiful.*

1. The Beautiful:—Difficulty of defining. Various theories. Two classes—objective and subjective. Subjective theories:—sensation; association; symbolism. Objective theories:—utility; order and proportion; unity and variety; the spiritual theory.

2. The Sublime:—Nature of sublimity; elements of sublimity; moral sublimity.

3. The Ludicrous:—Nature of the idea; nature of the ludicrous; forms of the ludicrous.

4. The power of Taste:—Its nature; its two elements; standard of taste, etc.

II. *The Culture of the Beautiful—(Æsthetic Culture).*

1. The value of the idea of Beauty:—To Character; to Literature; to the Arts; to Morality; to Religion; a source of enjoyment.

2. Culture of the Æsthetic nature:—From nature; from art; by literature; by music; by certain studies; the beautiful in character, etc.

3. Application in Teaching:—Condition of the school-room; pictures; flowers; music; poetry; drawing; manners of pupils, etc.

XIV. THE NATURE AND CULTURE OF THE RIGHT.

I. The Nature of the Good, or Right.

1. Nature of the idea of the Right:—The Right—Obligation—Merit and demerit. Origin of these ideas.

2. Theories of the nature of the Right :—Happiness ; utility; legal enactment; divine will, etc.; correct theory.

3. Origin of the idea of the Right:—Education; legal enactment; association; sympathy; Bain's theory; a moral sense; intuition.

4. Nature of Conscience :—Intellectual element; emotional element; their relation; what is conscience?

Nature of Ethics; diversity of moral judgments; is conscience a safe guide ?

II. The Culture of the Right—(Moral Culture).

1. Nature of this culture :—Ideas to be developed;—the right—obligation—merit and demerit. The idea of duty. The different duties.

2. Value of moral ideas :—To Literature; to the Arts ; to Character; to Society; to the State.

3. Principles of moral culture :—(a) Culture possible ; (b) should begin early ; (c) feeling with cognition; (d) in the concrete.

4. Methods of moral culture :—(a) By examples; (b) by literature; (c) by history ; (d) by the Bible ; (e) avoid evil influences ; (f) rules of moral action ; (g) moral habits; (h) moral ideals; (i) duty of parent and teacher, etc.

5. Application in Teaching:—Teachers should aim to develop the following:—

(*a*). Duties to self:—Self-control; purity; culture; industry; temperance; ambition; vanity; covetousness, etc.

(*b*). Duties to others:—Courtesy; obedience; veracity; honesty; charity; gratitude; patriotism, etc.

(*c*). Duties to God:—Faith; love; obedience.

NOTE.—In this brief discussion of the Right may be found the basis of a course in Moral Culture. A full treatment of the subject would embrace the Sensibilities and the Will.

THE SENSIBILITIES.

I. THE NATURE OF THE SENSIBILITIES.

Introduction:—The Sensibilities defined and illustrated. Relation to the intellect. Classification,—Emotions, Affections, and Desires. Duality of feelings. Other classifications.

I. The Simple Emotions.

The Emotions defined and illustrated. Classification,—Instinctive and Rational. Nature of each.

1. The Instinctive Emotions:—Cheerfulness and melancholy; companionship and loneliness; sympathy with happiness; sympathy with sorrow.

2. The Rational Emotions:—(*a*) The egoistic emotions,—pride and humility; (*b*) The æsthetic emotions:—novelty; wonder; beauty; sublimity; the ludicrous; (*c*) The ethical emotions:—obligation; satisfaction and remorse; approval or disapproval.

II. *The Affections.*

The Affections defined and illustrated. Classification, —Benevolent and Malevolent. Nature of each.

1. The Benevolent Affections :—Affection for kin-·dred ; friendship ; gratitude ; patriotism ; philanthropy ; piety.

2. The Malevolent Affections :—Resentment ; envy ; jealousy ; revenge, etc.

III. *The Desires.*

The Desires defined and illustrated. Their basis. Relation to aversion. Classification,—Physical and Rational.

1. The Physical Desires :—Food ; stimulants ; activ-·ity ; repose, etc.

2. The Rational Desires :—Happiness ; society ; wealth ; power ; esteem ; knowledge. Hope and fear.

II. The Culture of the Sensibilities.

1. Value of the Sensibilities :—Of great value ;—to the intellect ; to thought ; to will ; to literature ; to oratory ; to happiness ; to morality ; to religion.

2. General principles of their culture :—By judicious ·exercise ; develop the higher and repress the lower ; the law of moderation.

I. *Culture of the Emotions.*

1. The Instinctive Emotions :—Cheerfulness ; melan-·choly ; companionship ; sympathy.

2. The Rational Emotions :—Pride ; humility ; novelty ; beauty ; sublimity ; the ludicrous ; the moral feelings.

II. Culture of the Affections.

1. The Benevolent Affections:—Love of kindred; friendship; gratitude; patriotism; philanthropy; piety.

2. The Malevolent Affections:—Resentment; envy; jealousy; revenge, etc.

III. Culture of the Desires.

1. The Physical Desires:—Food; stimulants; activity; repose, etc.

2. The Rational Desires:—Happiness; society; wealth; power; esteem; knowledge.

———

THE WILL.

I. THE NATURE OF THE WILL.

Introduction.—General nature. Elements involved. Essential elements,—motive, choice, executive volition.

2. The Motive: — Definition; motive subjective; classes of motives; relation of desire and duty; relation of motive and cause.

3. The Choice:—Definition of choice; essential element; diversity of objects; liberty of selection; choice free; deliberation implied; the final decision.

4. The Executive Volition:—Its nature; relation to choice; when complete.

5. Remarks on the Will:—The will an active power; the will a cause; the conception difficult; Bain's philosophy of the will; Bain's view examined.

II. The Freedom of the Will.

1. The nature of freedom; a freedom from; a freedom to; "to do as we please," etc.

2. Arguments for freedom;—A general conviction; conscious of freedom; man's moral nature; consequences of the opposite, etc.

3. Objections to freedom:—Influence of sensibility; contrary choice; disposition; strongest motive; motives the cause; *dictum necessitatis;* Bain's views, etc.

III. The Culture of the Will.

1. Value of the Will :—To thought; to discovery; to oratory; to military success; to government; to religion; to courage; to character; to success in life.

2. Methods of cultivating the Will :—Stimulation; direction; self-control; overcoming obstacles; difficult studies; self-reliance; prompt decision; influence of other wills; moral influences.

BOOKS OF REFERENCE.—Baldwin's "Elementary Psychology ;" Brooks's "Mental Science and Mental Culture ;" Sully's "Hand-Book of Psychology ;" Preyer's "Development of the Intellect ;" Preyer's "Senses and the Will ;" Porter's "Human Intellect ;" Carpenter's "Mental Physiology ;" Herbart's "Psychology ;" Bain's "Mental Science ;" Spencer's "Principles of Psychology ;" Bain's "Moral Science ;" Bain's "The Senses and the Intellect ;" Bain's "The Emotions and the Will ;" Bain's "Mind and Body ;" Galton's "Natural Inheritance ;" Hamilton's "Lectures on Metaphysics and Logic ;" Mill's "Examination of Hamilton's Philosophy ;" Ladd's "Elements of Physiological Psychology ;" McCosh's "Psychology ;" McCosh's "Intuitions of the Mind, Inductively Investigated ;" Locke's "Essay on the Human Understanding ;" Lotze's "Outlines of Psychology ;" Calderwood's "The Relation of Mind and Brain ;" Galton's "Inquiries into Human Faculty and its Development ;" Ribot's "Diseases of Memory ;" Wood's "Brain-work and Over-work ;" James's "Principles of Psychology ;" Ribot's "The English Psychology ;" Carus's "The Soul of Man ;" Lindner's "Empirical Psychology ;" Kant's "Critique of Pure Reason ;" Todhunter's Logic ; Thomson's "Outline of the Laws of Thought ;" Jevon's Logic ; Hyslop's "Elements of Logic ;" Mill's Logic, etc.

PART II.

Methods of Instruction;

Or, the Science and Art of Teaching.

I. THE SCIENCE OF TEACHING.

I. THE GENERAL NATURE OF TEACHING.

1. Teaching defined. Relation to education. Its elements. Culture and Instruction.

2. Teaching a Science. Its claims to a science. Source of its laws and principles.

3. Teaching an Art. Its claims to an art. Source of its methods. The teacher an artist.

4. Teaching includes:—(*a*) The nature of mind; (*b*) The nature of knowledge; (*c*) The nature of instruction, its forms, order, and principles.

II. THE GENERAL NATURE OF THE MIND.

1. The Mind:—Its nature; how to study mind; its faculties.

2. General classification: — Intellect; Sensibility; Will. Their nature and relation.

3. The Intellect:—Perception; memory; imagination; understanding; intuition.

4. The Understanding:—Abstraction; conception; judgment; reasoning.

5. Other forms of mental activity:—Consciousness; attention, etc.

III. The General Nature of Knowledge.

1. Nature of Knowledge. Origin and development of knowledge. Relation of knowledge to the mind. Division of knowledge;—common knowledge—scientific knowledge —" inductive and deductive " knowledge—" empirical and rational "—the " formal sciences."

2. Classification of Knowledge:—Language; mathematics; physics; psychology; sociology; history; the arts.

3. The nature of each branch; its relation to the mind; origin of each branch; how developed.

4. Educational value of the studies:—Culture value; practical value; views of various authors upon the subject.

IV. The Forms of Instruction.

1. Nature of Instruction:—Instruction defined; relation to education; embraces,—forms, order, and principles.

2. Forms of Instruction: (a) analytic; (b) synthetic; (c) concrete; (d) abstract; (e) inductive (f) deductive; (g) theoretical; (h) practical.

3. The application of each form to the different branches of study explained.

V. The Order of Instruction.

1. The nature and value of this inquiry. Different periods require different studies and methods. Four educational periods,—infancy, childhood, youth, manhood.

2. Branches to be taught:—(*a*) in infancy; (*b*) in childhood; (*c*) in youth; (*d*) in manhood.

3. The same applied to the different grades of a public school.

VI. The Principles of Instruction.

1 The nature of principles; their value in teaching; three classes of principles; their origin; the application of the several principles to the different studies.

First Class—Principles Derived from the Nature of the Mind.

1. The primary object of teaching is to afford culture to the mind.

2. This culture should follow the natural unfolding of the powers of the child's mind.

3. The teacher should aim to give careful culture to the power of attention.

4. The teacher should aim to give careful culture to the perceptive powers of the child.

5. The teacher should aim to train the memory to operate by the laws of association and suggestion.

6. The teacher should aim to unfold the child's power of forming ideal conceptions.

7. The teacher should aim to give careful culture to the powers of abstraction and conception.

8. The teacher should take special pains to cultivate the judgment, or power of comparison, of the child.

9. A child should be taught to reason first inductively and then deductively.

10. A child should be led gradually to attain clear conceptions of intuitive ideas and truths.

NOTE.—These principles are to be explained and illustrated in the work of teaching.

Second Class—Principles Derived from the Nature of Knowledge.

1. The second object of teaching is to furnish the mind with knowledge.

2. Instruction should follow the natural order of the development of knowledge in the human mind.

3. The three principal sources of knowledge are observation, reflection, and language.

4. Things should be taught before words, and ideas should be taught before truths.

5. Particular ideas should be taught before general ideas, and particular truths before general truths.

6. The causes of facts should be taught before their laws, and causes and laws before scientific classifications.

7. The elements of the inductive sciences should precede the elements of the deductive sciences.

8. The formal study of the deductive sciences should precede that of the inductive sciences.

9. The elements of art should precede its related science, but advanced art must follow its related science.

10. The metaphysical or philosophical sciences should come last in a course of instruction.

Third Class—Principles Derived from the Nature of Instruction.

1. All instruction should seek to arouse the self-activity of the pupil.

2. The historic order of the development of knowledge is often suggestive of the proper order of instruction.

3. Elementary instruction should proceed from the simple to the complex, while advanced instruction may proceed from the complex to the simple.

4. Elementary instruction should proceed from the known to the related unknown, while advanced instruction may proceed from the unknown to the known.

5. Elementary instruction should be given in the concrete, while advanced instruction may be more abstract.

6. Both elementary and advanced instruction may be either analytic or synthetic, according to the nature of the subject.

7. Elementary instruction should be inductive, while advanced instruction may be deductive as well as inductive.

8. Elementary instruction should proceed from the practical to the theoretical, while advanced instruction may also proceed from the theoretical to the practical.

9. Elementary instruction should proceed from the conception of ideas or truths to their expression in language, while advanced instruction may also reach ideas and truths from their expression in language.

10. The arts are learned by intelligent doing, and the sciences by observation and experiment, language, and thinking.

NOTE.—It will be interesting to the teacher to note and discuss the principles of education presented by different writers. The principles given above are not designed to be exhaustive of the subject.

II. THE ART OF TEACHING.

1. The nature of art. Relation of art to science. How teaching is an art. Relation of the art to the science of teaching.

2. Teaching as an art includes :—1. The Elements of Knowledge; 2. Language; 3. Mathematics; 4. Physical Science; 5. History; 6. The Arts.

I. The Elements of Knowledge, or Object Lessons.

1. Their nature; origin of object lessons; value of the lessons; errors to be avoided.

2. The course of lessons:—1. On color; 2. On form; 3. On common objects; 4. On plants; 5. On animals; 6. On minerals; 7. On facts and phenomena of nature.

3. Method of giving the lesson. Model lessons on each of the above subjects.

Note.—For a fuller treatment, see the Elements of Science, page 47.

II. The Language Studies.

Introduction.—The nature of Language—Origin of spoken language—Origin of English language—Origin of written language—Value of language studies.

Subjects embraced.—1. Teaching to Read; 2. Orthography; 3. Pronunciation; 4. Reading or Elocution; 5. Grammar; 6. Composition; 7. Literature; 8. Lexicology.

I. Teaching a Child to Read.

1. *Nature of the Work:*—Written language—A source of knowledge—Its difficulties—Time to begin the work.

2. *Methods of Teaching:*—Several methods. (*a*) Alphabetic method; (*b*) Word method; (*c*) Sentence method; (*d*) Phonic method. Description and discussion of each.

3. *The Correct Method:*—Combination of word, sentence, and phonic methods.

Principles of the Method:—1. Begin with words and sentences rather than with letters.

2. Let the written word be regarded as a representation of the spoken word.

3. Pass from words to their elements, and use the elements to build up new words.

The Method Described:—(*a*) Words and sentences; (*b*) Analysis into elements; (*c*) New words from the elements; (*d*) General suggestions.

4. *The Child's Expression in Reading:*—(1). The child should get the thought.

(2). The child should make the thought its own.

(3). The child should express the thought as if it were its own.

(4). The child should thus read naturally as it speaks.

(5). All artificial methods of expression should be carefully avoided.

II. Teaching Orthography.

1. *Nature of Orthography:*—Its general nature—Its difficulty—Irregularity and its causes—Reform in spelling.

2. *Methods of teaching Orthography:*—Old methods— Modern methods—(*a*) The written method; (*b*) The oral method; (*c*) The spelling match.

3. *The Correct Method:*—State and discuss the principles and describe the methods.

Principles of Teaching:—(1). Teach first by writing words.

(2). The words should be written in sentences.

(3). Make use of common and familiar words.

(4). Cultivate the habit of observing the form of words.

(5). Impress mental pictures of words on the mind.

(6). Be careful not to impress misspelled words on the mind.

(7). Give attention to spelling in all the branches of study.

The Methods of Teaching:—The instruction should include the following:—

(1). Exercise in written spelling.

(2). Exercise in oral spelling.

(3). Names of common things.

(4). Words often misspelled.

(5). Associate words with one another.

(6). Give words to compose other words.

(7). Objections to the use of false orthography.

(8). Should rules of orthography be used?

III. Teaching Pronunciation.

1. *Its Nature.*—Nature of Pronunciation—Importance —Difficulty—Neglect—Standards, etc.

2. *Methods of Teaching.*—Different methods of teaching Pronunciation:—(1) The associative method—(2) The phonic method—(3) The alphabetic method—(4) The phonetic method.

3. *Correct Pronunciation.*—Pronunciation includes,— Articulation and Accent.

(1). Articulation:—Its nature; how to teach it; phonic analysis; errors of articulation.

(2). Accent:—Its nature; its principles; how to teach it; errors of accent.

IV. Teaching Reading or Elocution.

Introduction.—1. Nature of Reading—Its importance —Its neglect—A fine art.

2. Three elements :—the Mental element—the Vocal element—the Physical element.

3. General principles of teaching Reading:—(a) Natural expression; (b) Imitation of correct models; (c) Application of principles; (d) Correcting errors.

I. Teaching Primary Reading.

I. *The Mental Element.* Nature of the mental element—It includes :—(a) Comprehension; (b) Appreciation; (c) Conception.

1. *Comprehension:*—(*a*) Pupils should understand the meaning of words; (*b*) pupils should get the thought of the sentence; (*c*) pupils should state the thought in their own words; (*d*) pupils should analyze for prominent ideas; (*c*) the older pupils should study the reading lesson.

2. *Appreciation:*—(*a*) Pupils should feel the sentiment; (*b*) pupils should assimilate the sentiment; (*c*) the teacher should cultivate a taste for literature; (*d*) the sentiment should be adapted to the pupil.

3. *Conception:*—(*a*) Pupils should form mental pictures in reading; (*b*) abstract conceptions should be clear and vivid; (*c*) importance of the element of conception.

II. The Vocal Element. Nature of the vocal element —It embraces:—(*a*) Exercises in voice; (*b*) The use of the voice in reading.

1. Vocal Exercises:—(1) For vocal culture;—force, pitch, emphasis, etc.; (2) For correct pronunciation;—articulation, accent.

2. The Voice in Reading:—(1) Require natural expression; (2) Pupils should read as they talk; (3) If the talk is faulty correct it; (4) Secure correct rate, pitch, force, emphasis, melody, etc.

III. The Physical Element. 1. Nature of the physical element—What it includes—Its importance.

2. The Body in Reading:—Correct attitude—Position of the feet—Position of the hands—Holding the book—Turning the pages, etc.

II. Teaching Advanced Reading.

I. The Mental Element. 1. The Elements: (*a*) The Intellectual (comprehension); (*b*) The Emotional (appreciation); (*c*) Conception (in delivery).

2. Methods of Teaching:—Exercises—Natural expression—Principles—Correcting errors.

II. The Vocal Element. 1. The Elements:

(*a*). Quantity;—force, emphasis, stress.

(*b*). Compass;—key-note, slides, melody.

(*c*). Time;—rate, pauses, rhythm.

(*d*). Quality;—pure, orotund, tremulous, etc.

2. Methods of Teaching:—Exercises—Natural expression—Principles—Correcting errors.

III. The Physical Element. 1. The Elements:—
(*a*) Breathing—(*b*) Posture—(*c*) Gesture—(*d*) Facial expression.

2. Methods of Teaching:—Exercises—Natural expression—Principles—Correcting errors.

V. Teaching the Meaning and Use of Words.

1. *Nature of Subject.*—Nature of words—Origin of words—History in words—Value of words—Poetry in words—Change of words.

Methods of Teaching.—(1) By their use; (2) By reading; (3) By illustrations; (4) By definitions; (5) By synonyms; (6) Logical definitions; (7) Latin and Greek; (8) From etymology.

V. Teaching English Grammar.

Its Nature.—The nature of grammar—The grammatical elements—Origin of the elements—Historical development—Educational value—Practical value.

2. *Teaching Grammar.*—The teaching of grammar—Errors in teaching—Methods of teaching—Etymological method—Logical method—Comparison of the two methods.

3

3. *General Principles of Teaching.*—(1) Teach grammar from language and not from definitions; (2) Make the sentence the basis of grammatical instruction; (3) Make the subject practical to the learner.

I. Methods of Teaching Primary Grammar.

1. *Principles of Teaching :*—(1). Teach first the grammatical idea and then the expression of it.

(2). Lead pupils to discover the grammatical ideas.

(3). Do not teach mere expressions without ideas.

(4). Do not teach " grammatical forms " to young pupils.

2. *The Etymological Method :*—Description of the method :—(1) The parts of speech :—noun, verb, etc.; (2) The properties of parts of speech—number, person, etc.; (3) Classes of parts of speech :—of nouns; of verbs, etc.; (4) Exercises :—parsing; analysis; false syntax.

3. *The Logical Method.*—Description of the method :— (1) The Sentence ;—subject; predicate; copula; (2) The Elements :—principal; subordinate; limiting, etc.

4. *The Correct Method.*—A judicious and intelligent combination of the two methods.

II. Methods of Teaching Advanced Grammar.

1. *Grammatical Elements :*—Parts of speech; Classes of parts; Properties; Relations; Principles or rules.

2. *Formal Parsing :*—Its nature; Its value; Its object; Forms of parsing; Oral and written.

3. *Grammatical Analysis :*—Its nature; Its value; The method; Forms of analysis; Diagrams.

4. *False Syntax :*—Its object; Its value; The method.

VI. Teaching Composition.

1. *Its Nature.*—Nature of Composition—Its value; Errors in teaching.

2. Division of the subject for teaching :—(*a*) Primary composition; (*b*) Advanced composition.

I. Primary Composition (*Language Lessons*).

1. *Its Nature.*—Nature of language lessons : their value; neglect.

2. *Principles of Teaching :*—(1). Language is learned by imitation and practice.

(2). Language is learned by hearing good language.

(3). Language is learned by using good language.

(4). Language is learned by reading and committing good language.

(5). Use no rules or definitions with young pupils.

3. *Course of Lessons :*—(1). Give orally and in writing the names of objects, and their actions.

(2). Exercises in talking and writing sentences about various things.

(3). Have pupils talk about something, and then write what they have said.

(4). Look at objects and describe them, first orally, then in writing.

(5). Exercise in capital letters, elements of punctuation, etc.

(6). Reproduction of stories which have been told or read to the pupils.

(7). Have pupils read a selection, and then reproduce it, both orally and in writing.

(8). Look at pictures, and tell and write stories suggested by them.

(9). Exercises in letter-writing, notes of invitation and of acceptance, etc.

(10). Commit and recite choice selections of prose and poetry.

II. Advanced Composition.

1. *Preparation.*—1. Preparation for composition includes;—Materials—Words—Style of expression.

Source of Material.—Observation; reading; reflection; imagination, etc.

Source of Words.—Instinctive; imitation; general reading; conscious effort; the dictionary, etc.

Style of Expression.—Reading good authors; copying productions; committing prose and poetry; exercises in declamation, etc.

2. *Principles of Teaching:*—(1). The pupil should regard a composition as the expression of what he knows.

(2). Young pupils should begin with oral compositions.

(3). The transition should be made from oral to written compositions.

(4). A pupil's observation should be made the basis of his early composition.

(5). The imagination in inventing incidents should be early brought into exercise in composition writing.

(6). The power of reflection in arriving at truths and sentiments belongs to a latter stage of composition.

(7). The reading of suitable models of composition will both direct and stimulate original work in composition.

3. *The Writing of a Composition.*—It includes,—the subject, the material, the analysis, the amplification. Discussion of each.

(1). *The Subject*:—Its importance; adaptation; varied; how selected.

(2). *The Material.*—Observation; imagination; reflection; conversation; reading.

(3). *The Analysis.*—Leading ideas; subordinate ideas; arrangement; unity of thought.

(4). *The Amplification.*—Introduction; body; conclusion.

General Suggestions.—The written form; the corrections; the reading; literary exercises; newspaper in school, etc.

VII. TEACHING LITERATURE.

1. *Its Nature.*—The nature of literature; Ancient and modern; Value of the study; Classification of literary productions.

2. *Its Object.*—Objects in teaching literature :—(*a*) To impart a knowledge of literature; (*b*) To cultivate a taste for literature; (*c*) To secure skill in literary composition.

1. Primary Methods in Literature.

1. *Principles of Teaching :*—1. Begin with prose rather than with poetry.

2. Begin with the earlier forms of literature, as the fable, the fairy story, the historic narrative, etc.

3. Let the narrative or incident be the prominent thing considered with young pupils.

4. Have pupils reproduce orally the incidents heard or read.

5. Require pupils to invent stories, incidents, tales, etc.

6. Require pupils to commit and recite suitable extracts of prose and poetry.

2. *Methods of Teaching :*—1. List of works for young pupils to read; 2. The method of reading these works; 3. The method of conducting the exercises.

II. *Advanced Methods in Literature.*

1. *Principles of Teaching :*—1. Begin with the modern writers and proceed backward to the earlier ages.

2. Call attention to the fine sentiment and the noble characters of the literary productions.

3. Consider also the descriptions of natural scenery and the analysis of character.

4. Still later, the beautiful rhetorical figure and the artistic and felicitous use of language are to be noted.

5. Students should be required to commit and recite choice extracts or passages of prose and poetry.

6. Advanced pupils should make a critical study of literary productions, explaining historical and classical allusions, philosophical reflections, etc.

7. The ideal course should include all the master-pieces in literature from Homer to Tennyson.

2. *Methods of Teaching.*—List of authors to study; 2. Methods of studying these authors; 3. Method of conducting the recitation; 4. The cultivation of a love for literature.

III. THE MATHEMATICAL SCIENCES.

Introduction.—1. Nature of Mathematics. Branches of Mathematics;—arithmetic—geometry—algebra, etc.

2. The elements of mathematics:—Ideas,—Definitions. Truths,—Axioms—Theorems—Reasoning.

3. The value of mathematical studies :—Their practical value; their educational value.

I. TEACHING ARITHMETIC.

1. General nature of Arithmetic :—The nature of numbers. Origin of the idea. The decimal system of naming numbers. The Arabic system of writing numbers. A logical outline of arithmetic.

I. Teaching Primary Arithmetic.

1. *Introduction.*—Subjects to be taught :—(*a*) Ideas and language; (*b*) Elementary results; (*c*) Fundamental operations; (*d*) Elements of fractions; (*e*) Elements of denominate numbers.

2. *General principles of teaching primary arithmetic :*—

(1). The first lessons in numbers should be given orally.

(2). The first lessons in numbers should be given with objects.

(3). The method of teaching should be inductive.

(4). Mental and written exercises should be united.

I. Ideas and Expression of Numbers.—Nature of numerical ideas—Nature of the oral language of arithmetic—Nature of the written language.

1. *Principles of Teaching :*—(1). Use objects to develop the numerical ideas.

(2). Use groups of objects to develop the decimal method of numbering.

(3). Combine the figures so as to show the device of place value in writing numbers.

2. *Methods of Teaching.*—(*a*) Teaching the ideas and names; (*b*) Teaching the figures, and their combination. Describe in detail.

II. The Elementary Results.—Nature of elementary results. Methods of teaching the elementary results;— the old method; the Grube method; the Normal method.

1. *Principles of Teaching :*—(1). Teach addition and subtraction together.

(2). Teach multiplication and division together.

(3). Do not combine the four processes at first.

(4). Have pupils commit the elementary results of addition and multiplication.

(5). Lead pupils to derive the elementary differences from the elementary sums, and the elementary quotients from the elementary products.

2. *The Method :*—Addition and subtraction—Multiplication and division—Describe the method in detail.

III. The Fundamental Rules.—Nature of the fundamental rules—Relation to elementary results—The necessity of drill for facility and accuracy.

1. *Principles of Teaching :*—(1). Each process should be taught separately.

(2). Let the pupil see the reason for the methods of operation.

(3). Do not require pupils to commit rules for the operations.

(4). Drill pupils in the processes until they attain skill and accuracy in them.

2. *Method of Teaching.*—Addition; Subtraction; Multiplication; Division. Describe the method of teaching each.

IV. Elements of Denominate Numbers.—Nature of Denominate numbers—Irregularity of scales—Inconvenience—Metric system.

1. *Principles of Teaching :*—(1). Teach by means of the actual measures.

(2). Require pupils to make a practical application of the measures.

(3). Have pupils estimate length, distance, weight, etc.

2. *Method of Teaching :*—Length; Surface; Volume; Weight; Capacity, etc. Describe in detail.

V. The Elements of Fractions.—The nature of a Fraction—Its relation to the unit—The notation of fractions—Complexity of the conception of the notation.

1. *Principles of Teaching :*—(1). Develop the fractional ideas by means of objects.

(2). Pass from parts of a unit to parts of collections.

(3). Illustrate the processes with objects, lines, circles, squares, etc.

(4). Lead pupils to analyze the problems by reasoning from the unit.

(5). Derive the methods or rules by analysis and induction.

2. *Method of Teaching :*—(1). Introductory exercises :— (a) Parts of unit; (b) Parts of numbers; (c) Fractional expressions, etc.

(2). Reduction of Fractions:—(a) Numbers to fractions; (b) Fractions to numbers; (c) To higher terms; (d) To lower terms, etc.

(3). Addition and Subtraction :—(a) Denominators alike ; (b) Denominators unlike.

(4). Multiplication and Division:—(a) Fraction by number ; (b) Number by fraction; (c) Fraction by fraction ;

(5). The Relations of fractions :—(a) Fraction to a number; (b) Number to a fraction; (c) Fraction to a fraction.

NOTE.—A teacher should be able to show how to illustrate, analyze, and derive the rule in each one of these cases.

II. *Teaching Advanced Arithmetic.*

1. *The Course Includes.*—The course in advanced arithmetic includes the following subjects:—

1. Notation and numeration.
2. Fundamental rules.
3. Factoring and cancellation.
4. Divisors, multiples, etc.
5. Common fractions.
6. Decimal fractions.
7. Denominate numbers.
8. Percentage and interest.
9. Proportion, etc.
10. Involution and evolution.

2. *Methods of Teaching.*—For methods of teaching, see suggestions for grammar school course in arithmetic.

NOTE.—A teacher should be able to discuss the nature of each one of these subjects, and state the principles and describe the methods of teaching each.

III. General Suggestions.

1. *Mental Arithmetic:*—Its nature; its value; its abuse; methods of recitation, etc.

2. *Written Arithmetic :*—Its nature; forms of written work; methods of recitation, etc.

II. TEACHING GEOMETRY.

Introduction.—1. Nature of geometry—Divisions. Origin of geometry.

2. Value of geometry :—Educational value; practical value.

3. Things to be taught :—Geometrical ideas; Geometrical truths.

I. Teaching the Elements of Geometry.

1. *Nature of the Subject.*—Nature of the elements—Compared with arithmetic—Importance of teaching the elements to children.

2. *Principles of Teaching :*—

(1). The elements of geometry should precede the elements of arithmetic.

(2). The reasoning of geometry should follow the reasoning of arithmetic.

(3). The methods of teaching the elements should be concrete and inductive.

3. *Methods of Teaching :*—

The geometrical Ideas:—(1). The elements :—solid; surface; line; angle.

(2). Lines :—straight; curved; broken.

(3). Surfaces : — triangle ; quadrilateral ; parallelogram ; rectangle, etc.

(4). Solids:—cube; parallelopiped; pyramid; sphere; cylinder ; cone, etc.

(5). Angles :—acute ; obtuse ; right.

The geometrical Truths :—(1) Self-evident truths ; (2) Truths by concrete demonstration ; (3) Truths to be taken on faith.

II. Teaching Geometry as a Science.

1. *Nature of the Subject :*—(1). Definitions:—their nature —how to teach them.

(2). Axioms :—their nature—how to teach them.

(3). Demonstrations :—nature—kinds—errors—how to teach.

(4). Practical problems :—nature—importance—how to use them.

(5). Undemonstrated theorems :—nature—importance —how to use them.

2. *The Recitation in Geometry.*—(a) Assignment; (b) Construction ; (c) Demonstration ; (d) Criticism ; (e) Questioning; (f) Outlines, etc.

III. Teaching Algebra.

Introduction.—1. Nature of algebra. History of algebra; Relation to arithmetic. Symbols. Generalization. Algebraic reasoning. The equation. Deduction. Induction, etc. Mathematical induction, etc.

2. Value of the study :—Educational value ; practical value.

I. The Elements of Algebra.

1. *The Principles of Teaching :*—

(1). A careful transition should be made from arithmetic to algebra.

(2). Pupils should begin with concrete problems rather than with abstract exercises.

(3). Pupils should be led gradually to the process of generalization.

(4). There should be a thorough drill in all the processes.

(5). The interpretation of general formulas should be a prominent exercise.

2. *The Methods of Teaching.*—(*a*) Introduction; (*b*) notation; (*c*) negative quantity; (*d*) fundamental rules; (*e*) composition; (*f*) factoring; (*g*) fractions; (*h*) simple equations; (*i*) involution and evolution; (*j*) quadratic equations; (*k*) the progressions, etc.

3. *General Suggestions.*—(1) The literal notation; (2) Positive and negative quantities; (3) Exponents—general—negative—fractional, etc.; (4) Generalization—interpretation, etc.

IV. The Physical Sciences.

Introduction.—Nature of the physical sciences. Classification of the physical sciences. Elements of the physical sciences. Development of the physical sciences. Value of the physical sciences.

I. Teaching Geography.

1. *Nature of Geography :*—Divisions; origin; value,—educational—practical.

2. *Methods of Teaching Geography :*—(*a*) The synthetic method; (*b*) The analytic method; (*c*) The inductive method; (*d*) The deductive method.

3. *Courses in Geography :*—(*a*) Primary geography; (*b*) Advanced geography.

I. Teaching Primary Geography.

1. *Nature of the Subject.*—Nature of course in primary geography—What it embraces—When it should be begun.

2. *Principles of Teaching :*—(1). The first lesson in geography should be in the concrete.

(2). The course should be first synthetic then analytic.

(3). The facts should be presented before their classification or causes.

(4). The course should begin with local and descriptive geography.

(5). The course should combine history with geography.

3. *Methods of Teaching :*—(1). Perception of geographical facts :—Land ; water ; soil ; people, etc.

(2). Conception of geographical facts :—Land;—mountain ; prairie ; desert, etc. Water ;—lake ; river ; strait ; ocean, etc.

(3). Representation of geographical facts :—Direction ; making maps ; lessons on maps, etc.

(4). Explanation of geographical facts :—Form of earth ; motions of earth ; equator ; parallels ; meridians ; zones ; seasons, etc.

II. Teaching Advanced Geography.

1. *Nature of the Subject.*—General nature—Relation to primary course—Includes Descriptive and Physical.

2. *Principles of Teaching :*—(1). The method should be analytic as well as synthetic.

(2). The course should include the classification of facts.

(3). The course should include an inquiry into the causes of the facts.

(4). All possible devices should be employed to make the facts realistic to the mind of the student.

3. *Methods of Teaching.*—(*a*) Definitions; (*b*) descrip-, tions; (*c*) lessons on maps; (*d*) drawing maps; (*e*) interesting facts; (*f*) imaginary travels; (*g*) geographical outlines; (*h*) use of pictures, projections, etc.; (*i*) physical geography; (*j*) mathematical geography.

II. TEACHING PHYSIOLOGY.

1. *Nature of the Subject.*—Its general nature. Divisions for instruction. Value of the knowledge. Evils of ignorance. Relative importance of anatomy, physiology and hygiene.

2. *Principles of Teaching.*—(1). Instruction,—elements orally, advanced course with books. (2). Pupils learn,—by observation—by description—by drawing the parts. (3). Materials used,—the human body—parts of animals—plaster models—charts, etc.

3. *Elementary Course.*—(1). Anatomy and physiology:—Head—neck—trunk—arms—hands—legs—feet—bones—muscles—blood—heart, etc. (2). Hygiene:—Food—air—clothing—exercise—sunshine—sleep—bathing—nails—hair—eyes—ears—teeth, etc., effects of alcohol, etc.

4. *Advanced Course.*—(1). Subjects: — The bones — muscles—digestion—circulation—respiration—the skin—nervous system—organs of sense.

(2). Method:—Describe structure, use, laws of health, effect of alcohol and narcotics, etc.

III. THE ELEMENTS OF SCIENCE.

1. *Nature of the Elements.*—Object of this instruction; Value of this instruction. Subjects embraced;—plants—animals—minerals—air—water—heat—magnetism and electricity.

2. *Principles of Teaching :*—(1). Pupils obtain their knowledge from the object, and not from books.

(2). Pupils should be led to observe the phenomena of nature.

(3). Teacher should perform, and have pupils perform experiments.

(4). Pupils should describe objects through the language of words and drawing.

(5). Teacher should endeavor to cultivate an interest in the study of nature, her objects and forces.

3. *Course of Lessons :*—(1). PLANTS :—The leaf; the flower; various flowers; fruits; seeds; germination; growth; local flora.

(2). ANIMALS :—Starfish; sea-urchin; oyster; clam; snail; shells; lobster; crab; bee; grasshopper; cricket, etc; domestic animals; wild animals seen at the zoological gardens.

(3). MINERALS :—Quartz; feldspar; mica; hornblende; granite; puddingstone; slate; trap; marble; iron; copper; lead, etc.

(4). HEAT :—The flame—the candle—smoke—conduction—convection—radiation—simple experiments.

(5). AIR :—Its presence :—combustion; ventilation. Its pressure :—lifting-pump; force-pump; barometer; siphon. Elasticity of air :—the pop-gun; hydraulic fountain; air-brake; air-pump.

(6). WATER :—Its pressure :—equilibrium; fountains; artesian wells; city water system; hydrostatic press; elevators; cotton-presses. Capillarity :—tubes; blotter and ink; towel and water. Buoyancy :—boats; swimming; specific gravity.

(7). Electricity and Magnetism:—Frictional electricity; magnetism; dynamic electricity; the telegraph; the telephone, etc.; simple experiments.

Note.—For books of reference, see "Simple Experiments in the School-room," *J. F. Woodhull;* "Chemical History of a Candle," *Faraday;* "General History of Fire," *Tyler.*

V. Teaching History.

Introduction.—1. Nature of History; divisions; facts; philosophy, etc.

2. Value of the study of History:—educational value; practical value.

I. Teaching the Elements of History.

1. *Nature of the Subject.*—Nature of the elements of history—What should be embraced—The value of such lessons.

2. *Principles of Teaching:*—(1). The first lessons in history should be given orally.

(2). The first lessons in history should begin at home.

(3). The basis of instruction in the elements of history is biography.

(4). The first lessons in history should be given in the form of narratives.

(5). The elements of history should be taught in connection with geography.

3. *Methods of Teaching.*—The teacher's statement; the pupil's recitation; biography; historic narratives; home history; read histories; pupils bring historic matter into the school; use of blackboard and maps.

II. Teaching Advanced History.

1. *Nature of the History.*—Systematic ; style ; illustrations ; leading events ; historic centres ; cause and effect ; general history, etc.

2. *Students' Preparation.*—Use of the text-book ; books of reference ; use of a library ; original investigations ; graphic outlines, etc.

3. *The Recitation in History.*—Topical recitation ; order of recitation ; questioning ; new matter ; reviews ; discussions ; dates ; cause and effect ; maps and charts ; pupils make maps ; lectures, etc.

III. Civil Government, or Civics.

1. *Its Nature.*—Nature of civics. Value of a knowledge of civics.

2. *Methods.*—Course of instruction. Principles of instruction. Methods of instruction.

VI. The Arts.

Introduction.—Nature of Art—Its relation to science— The useful arts—The fine arts—Value of art—Educational value—The school arts,—writing, singing, drawing, etc.

I. Teaching Writing.

1. Principles of teaching.
2. Methods of teaching.

II. Teaching Vocal Music.

1. Value of vocal music.
2. Principles of teaching.
3. Methods of teaching.

4

III. Teaching Modeling.
1. Value of modeling.
2. Principles of teaching.
3. Methods of teaching: (*a*) in the solid; (*b*) in relief.

IV. Teaching Drawing.
1. Value of drawing.
2. Principles of teaching.
3. Methods of teaching: (*a*) surface drawing; (*b*) solid drawing.

V. Manual Training.
1. Nature and value of manual training.
2. Course of instruction in manual training.
3. Methods of instruction in manual training.

NOTE.—Special courses of instruction are being prepared for each one of the school arts and they are thus omitted in this general syllabus.

BOOKS OF REFERENCE.—Brooks's "Normal Methods of Teaching;" Bain's "Education as a Science;" Compayre's "Lectures on Pedagogy;" Currie's "Common School Education;" Fitch's "Lectures on Teaching;" Johonnot's "Principles and Practice of Teaching;" Page's "Theory and Practice of Teaching;" Prince's "Courses and Methods;" Parker's "Talks on Teaching;" Parker's "How to Study Geography;" King's "Methods and Aids in Geography;" Klemm's "European Schools;" Greenwood's "Principles of Education Practically Applied;" Raub's "Methods of Teaching;" Wickersham's "Methods of Instruction;" Hall's "Method of Teaching History;" Howland's "Practical Hints for Teachers of Public Schools;" Frye's "The Child and Nature;" White's "Elements of Pedagogy;" De Garmo's "Essentials of Method;" Patridge's "Quincy Methods;" Calderwood "On Teaching;" Rosmini's "Method in Education;" Shoup's "History and Science of Education;" Laurie's "Lectures on Language and Linguistic Method;" Prince's "Schools and Methods in Germany."

PART III.

School Economy.

Introduction.—Nature of the subject; what it embraces; the term school economy; other terms applied to the subject.

I. PREPARATION FOR THE SCHOOL.

1. *School Grounds.*—(*a*). Location:—convenient; suitable; healthful, etc.

(*b*). Arrangement;—size; shape; plan; apparatus.

2. *School Buildings.*—Size and form: internal arrangement; the basement; heating; ventilation; lighting, etc.

3. *School Furniture.*—Desks and seats; blackboards; blinds and curtains, etc.

4. *School Appliances.*—Text-books; charts; maps; globes; pens; pencils; slates; apparatus; specimens; library, etc.

5. *School Studies.*—For primary schools; for grammar schools; for high schools; for normal schools; for technical schools; for colleges.

II. ORGANIZATION OF THE SCHOOL.

1. *The Order.*—Admission; school hours; classification; the seating; intermission; communicating; signals, etc.

2. *The Studies.*—Text-books; formation of classes; assignment of classes to teachers; program of recitation; time for study, etc.

III. School Employments.

1. *Study.*—The objects; the incentives; modes of study; characteristics of a student; home study, etc.

2. *Recitation.*—The objects; the methods; teacher's preparation; pupil's preparation; reviews; examination; marking systems; graduation.

3. *Exercises.*—Plays; gymnastics; the Swedish system; the German system, etc.

IV. School Government.

I. School Duties.—To the pupils; to the teacher; to school property; to visitors, etc.

II. School Regulations.—To secure good conduct; to prevent misconduct; to correct misconduct.

III. School Punishments.—The object of penalties; principle of penalty; the kind of penalties; the method of punishments; improper punishments.

V. School Authorities.

I. The Teacher.—His qualifications; duties to pupils; duties to his profession; duties to the public.

II. School Officers.—Board of control; local boards; the superintendency.

III. The Patrons.—Their duties to the school; to the teacher; to their children.

VI. School Systems.

I. The American System.—Public schools; academies and seminaries; technical schools; colleges; universities, etc.

II. The German System.—The folks' school; the real schools; the gymnasia; the universities.

III. The French System.—The maternal schools; the elementary schools; the Lycée; the "Five Faculties."

IV. The English System.—Board schools; free schools; secondary schools; universities; technical schools.

Conclusion.

Relation of Education.—To labor; to health; to crime; to happiness; to government; to civilization.

Books of Reference.—Wickersham's "School Economy;" Raub's "Methods of School Management;" Baldwin's "Art of School Management;" Morrison's "Ventilation and Warming of School Buildings;" Kellogg's "School Management;" Landon's "School Management;" Payne's "Chapters on School Supervision;" Prince's "School Management, etc.;" Pickard's "School Supervision;" Newsholme's "School Hygiene;" Howland's "Practical Hints to Teachers;" Meyer's "Aids to Family Government," etc.

PART IV.

——

The History of Education.

——

I. INTRODUCTION.

Its place in a scheme of pedagogy. Its interest. Its value to teachers. What it embraces. Development of the individual—of science, art, and literature—of civilization. Methods of study.

II. ORIENTAL EDUCATION.

1. China:—The people; their character; religion; learning; system of education; influence of learned men; female education.

2. India:—Character of the people; religion; caste; learning; system of education; female education.

3. Persia:—Character of the people; religion; the magi; learning; system of education; female education.

4. Egypt:—Character of the people; caste; priests; learning; their arts; system of education; female education.

5. Judea:—Character of the people; religion; learning; literature; system of education; female education; influence on civilization.

III. GRECIAN EDUCATION.

1. The Greeks:—Their origin; character; language; literature; science; art; cause of their high development, etc.

2. Sparta:—Character of its people; its laws; system of education,—physical, intellectual, and moral education; female education.

3. Pythagoras (580 B. C.):—His life; his school; his system; his philosophy; his methods.

4. Athens:—Character of its people; its learning; literature; oratory; sculpture; architecture; system of education,—intellectual, physical and moral; female education.

5. Athenian Educators:—Socrates;—his life—character—methods of instruction; influence. Plato;—his life; works—philosophy—views on education—principles of instruction—influence. Aristotle;—his life—works—philosophy—views on education—principles of instruction—influence.

6. Alexandria:—The great library; The Septuagent. Teachers of science;—Euclid (fl. 300 B. C.)—Archimedes (287 B. C.); Apollonius (221 B. C.): Ptolemy (125 A. D.); Galen (fl. 130 A. D.); Hypatia (fl. 415 A. D.); Plutarch (40-120). Teachers of Christianity:—Polycarp—Ignatius—Justin Martyr—Origen, etc. Decline of Greek learning. Influence on the Romans.

7. Influence of Greek culture,—on science—on art—on education—on civilization.

IV. ROMAN EDUCATION.

1. The Romans:—Their origin; language; general characteristics; Grecian influence.

2. System of education:—Their schools; the teachers; *literator* and *literatus;* course of training; female education; influence of Greece.

3. Educational writers:—Cicero (106–43 B. C.);—his life—educational views. Seneca (12–69 A. D.);—his life—educational views. Quintilian (40–118 A. D.);—his life—works—educational views—system of instruction.

5. Influence of Roman culture on education and civilization.

V. Christianity and the Middle Ages.

I. Early Christianity.

1. Christ:—His education; life; character; as a teacher; His method; His doctrines; His influence.

2. Early Christians:—Their education; social life; home instruction; catechetical schools.

3. The Fathers of the Church:—Tertullian; St. Jerome; St. Augustine; their character; educational views.

4. Influence of Christianity on woman.

II. Education During the Middle Ages.

1. Decline of learning. Causes of the decline;—Opposition of Christianity to Greek literature—Destruction of the Alexandrian library—Fall of the Roman empire—Conquests of the Saracens—Asceticism. General ignorance.

2. Schools of the Church:—Monastic schools; cathedral schools; parochial schools; the seven liberal arts,—the *trivium* and *quadrivium*.

3. Charlemagne (768–814);—His interest in education; Alcuin (735–804).

4. Alfred the Great (848–901);—His interest in education; his studies and writings.

5. Chivalry;—Its rise; its influence on character; on social life; on education.

6. Rise of secular education; town or burgher schools.

7. Education of women.

VI. The Revival of Learning (12-15 C.).

1. Causes of the revival :—The Crusades ; Saracen learning; downfall of Constantinople (1453); study of classical literature; invention of printing; growth of spirit of freedom ; decline of feudalism : elevation of the middle classes.

2. Italy :—Literature ;—Dante (1265)—Petrarch (1304) —Bocaccio (1313). The Arts ;—Pisano (1208)—Giotto (1276)—Fra Angelico (1387)—Brunelleschi (1377)—Ghiberti (1381). Eminent teachers ;—Gerson (1363)—Vittorino (1379)—Æneas Sylvius (1405). Influence of Greek scholars ; establishment of libraries; University of Bologna (12 C.).

3. France :—The Troubadours ; the Trouvieres ; Abelard (1079) ; Scholasticism and " the seven liberal arts ; " Roscellinus (1092),—" nominalism and realism ; " the University of Paris (12 C.) ; Thomas Aquinus (1227) ; Froissart (1337).

4. England :—The Norman Conquest (1066); Le Franc (d. 1089) ; Anselm (d. 1109) ; Wickliffe (1324) ; Sir John de Mandeville (1300) ; Geoffry Chaucer (1328-1400) ; William Caxton (1412); Universities of Oxford and Cambridge (13 C.).

5. Germany :—The Minnesingers; the Master Singers; the Brethren of the Common Life (14 C); the Universities (14 C.) ; Thomas à Kempis (d. 1471).

VII. The Renaissance of the Sixteenth Century.

1. Meaning of the Renaissance. Progress in literature, art, and science. Study of ancient languages. Humanism in education. Causes of the Renaissance.

2. Italy (æsthetic education) :—Literature;—Lorenzo de Medici (1448)—Ariosto (1474)—Tasso (1544), etc. The Arts;—Leonardo da Vinci (1452)—Michael Angelo (1474)—Titian (1477)—Raphael (1483), etc. The Sciences; —Columbus (1435)—Galileo (1564)—Cardano (1501)— Tartaglia (1500), etc.

3. Germany :—The Humanists;—Agricola (1443)— Reuchlin (1455)—Erasmus (1467)—their educational works and views. Theological humanist;—John Sturm (1507)— his works—his school—his methods—his influence. The universities.

4. France :—Church Schools;—the schools of the Jesuits—their studies—methods of teaching—methods of discipline—their influence.

5. England (practical schoolmasters);—Lily (1468)— his grammar; Ascham (1515)—his "Scholemaster;" Mulcaster (1530)—his "Positions" and his "Elementarie; " Colet (1466).

6. The Reformation :—Wickliffe (1324) ; Erasmus (1467); Luther (1483); Melancthon (1497); Zwingli (1494); Calvin (1509); the influence of each on education; general educational influence of the Reformation.

VII. The Realists, or the New Education (Sixteenth and Seventeenth Centuries).

Reaction against abstract education; progress in science; progress in literature; intellectual emancipation.

1. France :—Rabelais (1483),—his life—writings— educational doctrines and influence. Montaigne (1533),— his life—writings—educational doctrines—influence.

2. England :—Bacon (1560),—his life—philosophy— writings—educational doctrines—influence on philosophy and education. Milton (1608),—his life—writings—educational views and influence.

3. Germany:—Ratich (1571),—his life—educational work—principles of teaching—influence.

4. Moravia:—Comenius (1592),—his life—educational work—writings—grades of schools—principles of teaching —influence on education.

IX. Education in the Seventeenth Century.

Progress slow; popular education not recognized; further planting of new ideas.

1. England:—Locke (1632),—his life—philosophy— educational doctrines—influence.

2. France:—Jansenism and Port Royal schools; their methods. Pascal (1628). Fenelon (1651),—his writings— educational views—labors. Rollin (1661),—his writings— labors—educational views.

La Salle (1651) (the Christian schools),—his life— character—labors—writings—educational views—teachers' seminary.

3. Germany:—Francke (1663),—his life—work— views—teachers' seminary—influence.

4. Education of women in the seventeenth century.

X. Education in the Eighteenth Century.

Progress in educational thought and practice; the methods of nature; growth of the idea of popular education.

1. France:—Rousseau (1712); the naturalistic school; his life—character—his Émilé—educational doctrines— his influence.

2. Germany:—Basedow (1723); the philanthropinist; his life — character — educational work — methods — influence.

3. Switzerland:—Pestalozzi (1746); life; character; educational experiments; his educational writings; educational views; merits and demerits; influence upon education.

4. The humanistic education; nature of humanism; representatives; their influence.

5. Education of women in the eighteenth century.

X. Education in the Nineteenth Century.

The golden age of education; general adoption of new ideas; recognition of the principle of popular education; establishment of public schools; college education modified; female education provided for; establishment of normal schools, etc.

1. Switzerland:—Pere Girard (1765),—his life—educational work—educational doctrines—educational influence.

2. France:—Jacotot (1770),—his life—his doctrines—his influence. Madame de Genlis; Madame Guizot; Madame Necker, etc. The Natural Schools.

3. Germany:—Froebel (1782),—his life—educational labors—educational doctrines—the kindergarten—influence on education. The State Schools.

4. England:—Bell; Lancaster; Wilderspin; Stow; Hannah Moore; Dr. Arnold. System of schools.

5. America:—Horace Mann; Cyrus Pearce; David P. Page; Warren P. Colburn; Mary Lyon; Emma Willard, etc. The Public Schools.

XI. Recent Educators.

French:—Saint Simon; Fourier; Comte; Dupanloup; Buisson; Compayré.

German:—Herbart; Beneke; Dressler; Grube; Schmidt.

English :—Herbert Spencer; Alexander Bain; J. G. Fitch; R. H. Quick; S. S. Laurie.

American :—Henry Barnard; Thomas H. Burrows; James P. Wickersham; John D. Philbrick, etc.

XIII. History of Education in the United States.

Public schools :—their origin ; origin in Pennsylvania ; in Philadelphia.

Colleges and Universities :—their origin; growth; eminent men connected with them, etc.

Normal schools : their origin ; development; eminent men connected with them.

Female education : seminaries ; women's colleges ; admission into men's colleges, etc.

Teachers' Institutes : State Teachers' Association ; National Educational Association; The National Bureau of Education.

XIV. Contemporary Public Education.

In Germany : the primary schools ; the gymnasia ; the real schools ; the universities.

In France : maternal schools ; elementary schools ; lyceums ; the " Five Faculties."

In England : board schools ; free schools ; endowed schools ; universities.

Books for Study and Reference.

General Histories.—Painter's " History of Education ; " Compayre's " History of Pedagogy ; " Browning's " Educational Theories ;" " History and Progress of Education," by Philobiblius; Quick's " Educational Reformers ; " Hallman's " History of Pedagogy."

Special Treatises.—Laurie's " Rise of Universities ; " Laurie's. " Comenius : " Barnard's " German Teachers and Educators ;" Staunton's " Schools of England ; " Morley's " Rousseau ;" " Rousseau's Émilé," by W. H. Payne ; De Guimp's " Pestalozzi ;" Krüsi's " Life of Pestalozzi ;" Pestalozzi's " Leonard and Gertrude ;" Leitch's " Practical

Educationists;" Joseph Payne's Lecture on Jacotot in "Lectures on the Science and Art of Education;" Gill's "Systems of Education;" "Reminiscences of Froebel," by Von Marenholz-Bulow;" "Memoir of Froebel," Milton Bradley & Co.; Hailman's "Kindergarten Culture;" Froebel's "Education of Man;" "Free School System in the United States," Charles Francis Adams; Wickersham's "History of Education in Pennsylvania;" Boone's "History of Education in the United States;" Helene Lange's "Higher Education of Women in Europe;" Joseph Payne's "Visit to German Schools;" Matthew Arnold's "Report on Schools of France and Germany," and "Higher Schools and Universities of Germany;" Klemm's "Visit to European Schools;" Bardeen's "French Schools through American Eyes;" Grasby's "Teaching in Three Continents;" Mullinger's "History of the University of Cambridge;" Lyte's "History of the University of Oxford;" Draper's "Intellectual Development of Europe;" "Ignatius Loyola," by Hughes; "The Jansenists," by Sainte Beuve.

WORKS FOR GENERAL READING.—Mahaffy's "Old Greek Education;" Church's "Roman Life in the Days of Cicero," Chapters I and II; Stillé's "Studies in Mediæval History," Chapters XII, XIII, XIV; Maitland's "The Dark Ages;" Gibbon "Student Edition," Vols. II and III; Mullinger's "History of the Schools of Charles the Great;" Townsend's "Great Schoolmen of the Middle Ages;" Stubbs's "Lectures on Mediæval and Modern History," Chapters VI and VII; Conde's "The Arabs in Spain;" Symond's "Renaissance in Italy;"—"The Revival of Learning;" Pater's "The Renaissance;" Green's "Shorter History of the English People," Chapters I, II, III, VI."

FOR CONTEMPORARY EDUCATION.—See Reports of the U. S. Commissioner of Education, Department of the Interior.

It would be well for students of the history of education to read in connection with the subject some good general outline of the history of Europe, as Freeman's "General History of Europe." Barnard's "Journal of Education " is a rich mine of information on the history of systems and methods. The article on Education in the " Encyclopædia Britannica is a valuable monograph upon the subject. Bohn's Editions of Plato, Aristotle, and Quintilian are also recommended; especially Plato's "Republic," Aristotle's " Politics and Economics " and Quintilian's "Institutes of Oratory."